The Best Birthday Present

Written by Virginia King
Illustrated by Mitch Vane

Nicky opened his birthday present
from Jake.
"Wow, look at this!" he said.
"Gee, thanks Jake."

Jake had made Nicky a huge picture
of a steam train. But it wasn't just a flat
picture. Somehow Jake had cut around
all the doors and windows so that
they opened up.

Nicky ran his fingers along the picture, opening all the doors and looking at the people inside.

There was even a door on the engine, so that Nicky could see the driver.

"This is terrific, Jake!" said Nicky.
"I always like your presents the best.
You make such great things."

To
Nicky
Love
Jake

Jake wheeled himself over and punched
Nicky on the arm.
"I like making things for my little brother,"
he said.

Then Nicky said to Jake, "The trouble is, it's *your* birthday soon, and I'm hopeless at making things."

"Don't worry," said Jake. "Anything will do."

But Nicky wanted to give Jake something
really special.
"Just like the presents he gives me,"
Nicky said to himself.

So Nicky started thinking.

He thought while he was in bed at night.

He thought while he was eating breakfast.

He thought while he was taking a bath.
What could he give Jake that would
be really special?

"Perhaps I *could* make something,"
Nicky thought to himself.

"How about a model helicopter?"

No, Jake could make a better helicopter
for himself. Anyway, where would Nicky
get the money to buy the kit?

Everything Nicky thought about making,
Jake could make better for himself.

Nicky asked his mother if she had
any ideas.

"Maybe you could take Jake out for his
birthday," she said. "You could take
a special picnic lunch to the park.
There might be a football game
that you could watch."

"Mmmm," said Nicky. But he knew that
Jake was tired of watching people play
football.

"Let's make him a special cake," said his mother, "in the shape of a spaceship or something."

"Maybe," said Nicky. But he knew that Jake was too old for spaceships.

Every day, Jake's birthday got closer, and every day Nicky tried to think of a good present.

Finally, he asked Grandma.

Grandma listened carefully.

Then she said,
"Well, the first thing you have to do is stop worrying about it. Just trust yourself, Nicky. You'll think of something. You'll think of something."

So Nicky stopped worrying, but he didn't stop thinking.

One week before Jake's birthday, Nicky
went for a walk to Dr. Evans' farm.

Dr. Evans had pigs and ducks and chickens.
Maybe there'd be some eggs to collect.
And maybe the walk would help him think.

When he got there, Nicky was surprised to see Dr. Evans grooming a horse.

"Hi Nicky," called Dr. Evans.
"What do you think of my new horse?
Her name's Thunder."

"She's beautiful," said Nicky.
"So golden and shiny!"

"She's friendly, too," replied Dr. Evans.
"She's as gentle as a lamb."

Nicky patted Thunder on the nose, and looked up at her dark, gentle eyes.

Dr. Evans said, "You can help me brush her if you like."

Nicky used a big brush and Thunder snorted as if she was enjoying it.

"How's Jake getting along?"
asked Dr. Evans. "Maybe he'd like
to meet Thunder, too."

Nicky began to think.

Dr. Evans said that Nicky could brush
Thunder every afternoon. He showed
Nicky how to feed her, too.

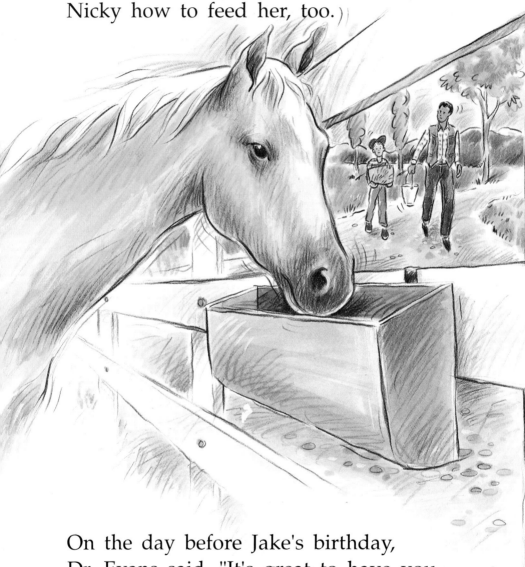

On the day before Jake's birthday,
Dr. Evans said, "It's great to have you
help me look after Thunder. I'll have
to think of something that I can do
for you."

"Well," said Nicky . . .
"Maybe you can help me give Jake
a special birthday present."

"Where are we going?" asked Jake,
as Nicky pushed him down the track
the next day.

"You'll see," said Nicky, smiling to himself
with excitement.

Jake looked surprised when they stopped
at Dr. Evans' farm.

"I didn't know Dr. Evans had a horse," he said.

"Her name's Thunder," said Nicky, "and she's going to give you your birthday present."

Dr. Evans said, "Are you ready to go for a ride, Jake?"

Jake opened his eyes really wide, and then he nodded his head.

Dr. Evans lifted Jake out of his wheelchair
and onto Thunder's back.
"Hold onto the saddle tightly," he said.

Nicky put Jake's feet into the stirrups.
Thunder snorted.

Jake still didn't say anything,
but Nicky watched his face.
Dr. Evans led Thunder and Jake
around and around the yard — slowly
at first, and then a little faster.

Jake looked nervous for a moment or two, but soon he started to smile, and suddenly he laughed out loud.

"This is great!" Jake yelled, and then
he looked down at his little brother.
"Thanks Nicky! This is the *best* birthday
present ever."